TRUST YOURSELF, YOU ARE AMAZING

The Adventures of Amelie

by MILL SNOWS

www.WeAreAllAmelie.com

First Edition. February 2023

ISBN: 9798378339082

Sello: Independently published

DISCOVER THE ADVENTURES OF AMELIE!

A book full of short stories that will inspire you to have courage, friendship, inner strength, and much more.

This collection of fictional tales based on everyday life will allow you to delve into a world full of adventures, overcoming challenges, teamwork, self-confidence, and family values.

Each chapter will leave you with a lesson and at the end of each one, you will find an activity to reinforce the concepts learned. An easy-to-read book ideal for girls and young people looking for inspiration and empowerment.

Don't miss the opportunity to get this book and live incredible adventures with Amelie!

Written by MILL SNOWS

The Adventures of Amelie

The Adventures of Amelie

INTRODUCTION

Hey! I'm Amelie, a girl just like you and your friends. I love to have everyday adventures that present me with many challenges that I have to overcome. With the help of my family and friends, I always solve different challenges that teach me many things. In this book, you will find very easy to read short stories that will make you feel identified.

I hope you like them and enjoy reading them!

The Adventures of Amelie

TRUST YOURSELF

Amelie is a curious and very adventurous girl who lives in a small town surrounded by mountains and forests. She lives with her parents in a not very big, but very cozy house on the main street of her town, just a few meters from a river and a beautiful forest where she usually spends a lot of time living amazing adventures alone or with her friends.

One day, while walking through the forest, she discovered a path she had never seen before. With her heart beating with excitement and her eagerness to explore, she did not hesitate for a minute and decided to follow that path to see where it led. She took her compass so as not to get lost and set out on the road to her new adventure.

After walking for a long time observing nature, she came to a clearing in the middle of the forest and in the center there was a giant, ancient tree with large branches and many leaves. Looking up, she saw a nest at the top. She decided to approach the tree and discovered that there was a wounded bird in the nest. From below, she heard the bird's cries of pain, which made Amelie feel distressed immediately and without thinking twice, she decided to help it.

But when she tried to climb the tree, she realized that it was much higher than it seemed. However, Amelie did not let fear defeat her and found a way to climb. She trusted herself and slowly, holding onto the strongest branches, with a lot of mental and physical effort, but always with great caution, she climbed the tree.

Once on top, Amelie took the bird in her hands and saw that it had a hurt wing. She carefully lowered it and began to nurse it. She cared for it for a few hours until it was strong enough to fly. The bird was ready and could return home, no longer in pain, and as a symbol of gratitude, it gave Amelie a golden feather as a reminder of her adventure. She very excitedly stored it in a very cute wooden box that she always carries with her in her backpack, where she treasures memories of her adventures.

She calls it her "lifebox" because it holds memories of her life.

Amelie returned to her town with the golden feather as a trophy from her adventure, very happy to have helped the bird and with a lot of confidence in herself. From that day on, Amelie continued to explore the world and live incredible adventures.

ACTIVITY

Write here if you have a special box or place where you keep memories from your life.

. . . .

. . . .

. . . .

. . . .

. . . .

. . . .

. . . .

. . . .

. . . .

. . . .

. . . .

. . . .

. . . .

. . . .

COLOR AND DECORATE

Get inspired by other creations on social media using #WEAREALLAMELIE.

I TRUST MYSELF.

I AM AMAZING.

COLOR

Get inspired by other creations on social media using #WEAREALLAMELIE.

Designed by Freepik

ACCEPT HELP

One hot summer morning, Amelie was playing in the river near her village when she suddenly saw something shiny at the bottom. With her adventurous spirit, she ran to get her diving goggles, took a big breath of air at the surface, and dove in. She began to descend, never taking her eyes off the shiny object. When she reached the bottom, she discovered it was an old glass chest that shone in the sun and looked very valuable.

But when she tried to pick up the box, she realized it was trapped in a net of algae and branches. Amelie worked hard to free the chest, but the more she worked, the more tangled it became.

Suddenly, she heard a strange noise and saw a group of fish approaching. Amelie was very scared, thinking the fish would attack her, but then she discovered that the fish were friendly and wanted to help her free the chest.

Together, Amelie and the fish, after much effort and perseverance, managed to rescue the chest and bring it to the surface. When she opened it, she discovered it was full of wonderful treasures and a note that read: "These treasures are for those who have the courage to venture, the humility to accept help and find them."

Amelie was excited and grateful for her adventure in the river. She hurried back to her village and told her friends about her adventure with the friendly fish.

Since that day, Amelie always remembers that courage, determination, and the humility to accept help can take her to incredible places.

ACTIVITY

Write here if you have ever rejected someone's help because you thought something bad about that person without getting to know them first.

. . . .

. . . .

. . . .

. . . .

. . . .

. . . .

. . . .

. . . .

. . . .

. . . .

. . . .

. . . .

. . . .

. . . .

COMPLETE, COLOR AND DECORATE

Get inspired by other creations on social media using #WEAREALLAMELIE.

I ACCEPT HELP

WITHOUT PREJUDICE

NEVER GIVE UP

One Saturday afternoon while Amelie was playing in the attic of her house, she discovered an old chest filled with dust. Her curiosity got the best of her and she decided to open it. She gently brushed off the dust and opened it. Inside were piles of old family memories, but one thing caught her attention - a brown leather notebook with a red ribbon tying it closed. On the cover was an inscription that read "Anton's Adventure Log."

Amelie was moved to tears - it was her great-grandfather's childhood adventure book and it had been in that chest for over a hundred years. As soon as she opened it, she was moved by the many adventures that were written in that notebook, but what intrigued her the most was a map that showed the location of a supposed hidden treasure. Amelie was ecstatic about the discovery and her adventurer's instinct made her not hesitate for a minute to follow the map to find the treasure.

The path led her to the mountain near her town. It was not an easy journey to get there. Amelie had to overcome many obstacles such as crossing a river, climbing a mountain, and avoiding traps. But she was determined to find her great-grandfather's treasure.

After a long journey, Amelie arrived at the point marked on the map - a small and somewhat dark cave. She turned on her flashlight and bravely entered. At the end of the cave, she found a chest decorated with many colors on the outside. When she tried to open it, she discovered that it was sealed with a magical key.

Amelie did not give up and continued to search for the key. She finally found it hidden under a rock behind a bush next to the cave entrance.

Amelie was able to open the chest. But what was inside was not gold coins or precious stones. Instead, there were her great-grandfather's personal treasures - a letter he wrote to his childhood love and never had the courage to give her, an old photo of his father and mother, tickets from a cruise he took with his family, a green and purple feather pen, a few worn crystal marbles, and an old silver pocket watch.

Amelie returned home to tell her parents how excited and grateful she was for the adventure she had experienced and for having found her great-grandfather's most precious treasure.

ACTIVITY

Write down the 10 things that you consider your most cherished treasures.

1. ....

2. ....

3. ....

4. ....

5. ....

6. ....

7. ....

8. ....

9. ....

10. ....

HELPING HELPS YOU

It was very early, a spring morning, when Amelie was walking through the forest and suddenly heard a strange sound. It was like a cry or a whimper, but she couldn't identify it. As she investigated, she discovered it was a beautiful fox lying on the grass, apparently injured. Despite being afraid that the little fox could attack her, Amelie decided to help it. She thought about how to pick it up without causing further harm. She decided to cover it with a blanket she had in her backpack, picked it up and took it to her house to clean and heal it.

However, when Amelie tried to heal it, she discovered it needed special medicine that she didn't have. Amelie had two options, the first was to wait for her parents to come back from work and take the fox to a vet in the city, which was an hour away from her town, or the second was to go to the mountain to find the medicine. Amelie knew from her grandparents that she could find some medicinal herbs in the mountain that would surely help the fox.

The first option was not possible, as it would take many hours until the vet could see the fox at night, and there was a risk that the fox would get worse. The second option had an extra challenge for Amelie, which was to overcome her fear of the mountain.

Amelie chose the second option, facing her fear of the mountain without fear of failure. The mountain was full of dangers, such as wolves and cliffs, but

Amelie didn't give up and continued her journey.

After walking for an hour, she arrived at the place where she found the medicine. She quickly collected it, put it in her backpack and began the journey back home.

Finally, Amelie healed the fox and released it back into the forest.

Amelie was excited and proud to have helped the fox and overcome her fears of the mountain.

ACTIVITY

Write your favorite name for the fox::

. . . .

. . . .

. . . .

. . . .

COMPLETE THE DRAWING AND COLOR

Get inspired by other creations on social media using #WEAREALLAMELIE.

Designed by Freepik

THE POWER OF FRIENDSHIP

Amelie was walking through the village when she met two new friends, a boy named Lucas and a girl named Sofia. They all shared the same passion for adventure and exploration, so they decided to join forces and go on an adventure together.

They planned to meet early on Sunday by the river. The three children knew a legend about an old abandoned village that was in the middle of the forest. According to urban legend, the village was enchanted and possessed ancient relics that no one had been able to rescue.

That Sunday, as soon as it dawned, the three friends got together and with backpacks full of water, food, and material for the expedition, set out on their adventure. They walked for hours in the forest until they found the village. There were no people, the houses were empty but in good condition. It seemed that by magic the village had been preserved in time but without people.

When they entered the old bank, they saw the vault open and thought that the treasure would no longer be there, but as soon as they approached the reflection of the relics, some gold coins, they were dazzled by their shine. Quickly they jumped in as if it were a swimming pool, and swam very excitedly among the coins.

When Lucas tried to take some coins out of the vault, he saw how they vanished in his hands. Very surprised, he understood that it was indeed a magical village and that treasure was there to stay forever. You could see and touch it, but only inside the vault. The legend was true.

The three children returned home very happy with their adventure and with a very valuable treasure, "friendship forever". Amelie was grateful for having met her new friends and for having lived an exciting adventure together.

ACTIVITY

Write the names of your friends:

....

....

....

....

....

....

....

COLOR AND DECORATE

Get inspired by other creations on social media using #WEAREALLAMELIE.

FRIENDSHIP

Designed by Freepik

OVERCOMING FEARS

Amelie had always been afraid of heights, which prevented her from exploring some exciting places. But one day, she heard about a beautiful place with the best views of the nearby valley. It could only be reached by climbing some rocks on the mountain.

Despite her fear, Amelie decided to face it and climb the rocks to reach the beautiful place. During the ascent, Amelie got scared many times and thought about descending, but with the help of her bravery and determination, she managed to overcome her fears and reach the top.

Amelie only visualized success, nothing could stop her, every time she doubted or felt fear she visualized herself at the top and so she could keep moving forward.

Once at the top, Amelie discovered a beautiful garden of flowers and bright butterflies that only live there, as well as beautiful views of the valley where her village is located. She understood that the effort to see that beautiful place was worth it.

From that moment on, Amelie left her fear of heights behind and continued to explore exciting places. She was proud of having overcome her fear and discovering that wonderful place.

ACTIVITY

Visualization exercise. Write a list of your main fears. Once written, read one aloud and create a mental image of yourself overcoming the challenge.

Example: "I'm afraid of the water."

Then, you create a positive image in your mind of yourself swimming freely in the sea or the pool and enjoying that moment.

Repeat this daily with each of your fears.

Some benefits of visualization:

1.Facing negative emotional states such as anxiety or stress.
2.Promotes relaxation of your body and sleep.
3.Enhances imagination.

COMPLETE THE DRAWING AND COLOR

Inspírate con otras creatividades en redes sociales usando el #SOMOSTODASAMELIE

Designed by Freepik

TEAMWORK

Amelie and her classmates went on a field trip to a national park very close to their school. Along the way, they realized that the path was blocked by a flooded river and a broken bridge.

Without knowing how to cross the river, Amelie and her classmates decided to work together and overcome the obstacles. Each one contributed their unique skills and talents to build a temporary bridge to cross the river.

Some provided ideas, those who were good at drawing made the plans, Amelie, who is good at math, did the calculations, some looked for materials, and others who are skilled at creating things were the builders.

After much teamwork and effort, they managed to build the bridge and continue their excursion. But soon they encountered another obstacle, a high rock wall that prevented them from continuing.

Amelie and her classmates did not give up and worked together to find a solution. With the help of harnesses and a rope, they managed to climb the rock wall and continue on their way.

At the end of the field trip, the children returned home with a great sense of achievement for having overcome the obstacles together. Amelie was happy to have had an exciting adventure with them.

ACTIVITY

Make a list of your friends' skills to consider on your next excursion.

1.Name: .... Skills: ....
2.Name: .... Skills: ....
3.Name: .... Skills: ....
4.Name: .... Skills: ....
5.Name: .... Skills: ....
6.Name: .... Skills: ....
7.Name: .... Skills: ....
8.Name: .... Skills: ....
9.Name: .... Skills: ....
10.Name: .... Skills: ....
11.Name: .... Skills: ....
12.Name: .... Skills: ....
13.Name: .... Skills: ....
14.Name: .... Skills: ....
15.Name: .... Skills: ....
16.Name: .... Skills: ....
17.Name: .... Skills: ....
18.Name: .... Skills: ....
19.Name: .... Skills: ....
20.Name: .... Skills: ....

COLOR AND DECORATE

Get inspired by other creations on social media using #WEAREALLAMELIE.

Designed by Freepik

TOGETHER IS BETTER

Amelie and her best friend, Mateo, decided to venture into the forest behind their house.

Mateo is the most loving person Amelie had ever met in her life, he had been diagnosed with Autism Spectrum Disorder, a condition related to brain development and sometimes had difficulties with communication, social interaction and needed his time to overcome some challenges.

However, Amelie was always there to help Mateo

and make sure he felt included and valued. Together, they explored the forest, looking for new places and discovering unknown animals and plants.

But soon, they encountered an obstacle. A river was in their way and there was a hanging bridge that moved a lot and its planks were very separated that at the slightest distraction, one could slip a foot. Mateo began to feel overwhelmed and lose confidence in himself.

Amelie, who had been in similar situations before and knew it was important to help Mateo overcome this obstacle, so together they found a solution. With a rope tied around their waists, Amelie went first across the bridge showing Mateo where to place each step. And so Mateo followed Amelie's steps until he crossed the bridge.

Mateo was proud of himself for overcoming this

obstacle and Amelie was happy to have helped her best friend feel safer and more confident.

That same day they continued their adventure in the forest and found new exciting places and challenges that they were able to overcome together.

ACTIVITY

Write down the challenges you overcame with your friends in the past year.

....

....

....

....

....

....

....

....

....

COLOR AND DECORATE

Get inspired by other creations on social media using #WEAREALLAMELIE.

Designed by Freepik

NO MORE SCHOOL BULLYING

Amelie had noticed that several of her classmates were being bullied and harassed by a group of older students at school. This worried her a lot and she wanted to do something about it.

One day, while she was in the schoolyard, she saw John, one of her classmates, being mistreated. Amelie decided to act immediately and approached John to ask if he was okay.

John, told her everything that had been happening

and Amelie felt furious. She knew she had to do something to stop the bullies and protect her classmates.

So, with courage and determination, Amelie confronted them and told them that they had to stop the school bullying immediately. They started laughing at her, but Amelie kept going and insisted that what they were doing was wrong and physically and mentally harmful to others.

At first, these kids didn't want to listen, but Amelie didn't give up. She talked to them about the importance of being kind and respectful to others and made them see and understand the negative consequences of their behavior.

Finally, the embarrassed young people understood and promised to stop their bad behavior. Amelie had managed to dissuade them and protect her schoolmates.

Some useful tips:

When you see or witness a case of school bullying:

1.Talk to a parent, teacher, or other trusted adult and tell them what's going on. re.

2.Be kind to the person who is being bullied. Show them your interest by trying to include them. Simply spending time with them will help them know that they are not alone.

Keeping quiet makes things worse. The person who engages in school bullying will think it's okay to continue mistreating others.

COLOR AND DECORATE

Get inspired by other creations on social media using #WEAREALLAMELIE.

ASKING FOR HELP IS GOOD

Amelie and her friends from the village were excited to go on a mountain hike. They had planned everything carefully and were ready for a day of adventure. However, once they reached the top, it started to snow heavily, obstructing their way back.

Amelie realized that the situation was getting more and more dangerous. The snow was falling harder and the daylight was beginning to diminish. If they didn't find help soon, she and her friends could freeze on the mountain

So she decided to take action. But she couldn't solve it alone. She was a little scared, but she didn't want to let her friends be in danger. With courage, she left her friends under the protection of an improvised shelter and embarked on a dangerous path to ask for help.

The way down was difficult. The snow was falling heavily and there were many obstacles in her way, but Amelie kept going, never losing hope. Finally, after a long walk, she arrived at a small village halfway down the mountain.

With the help of a group of kind people, Amelie was able to organize a rescue team to help her friends.

Together, they managed to reach the top of the mountain and rescue her friends just in time, before it got dark and the cold became unbearable.

Amelie felt very proud of herself and her friends thanked her for her courage and leadership. From that day on, they learned to value their friendship even more, to respect and help each other in times of need.

Remember:

"Asking for help makes us more honest when we have to help others. Asking for help has nothing to do with failure, dependence, or low self-esteem. Seeking help is about recognizing your limitations, humility, and courage"

DISCOVER THE DIFFERENCES

Mark with an X the 10 differences between the two images.

Designed by Freepik

KINDNESS AND GOODNESS EXIST

One winter day, Amelie decided to take a walk in the snowy mountain, she wanted to explore and discover everything she could.

After a while of walking among the trees, it started to snow, and in a few minutes the snowfall became more intense and began to fall harder. Amelie, desperate, quickened her pace along the trail to try to find shelter. Suddenly, she saw a light in the distance, an old house, and decided to approach it.

Amelie approached cautiously, not knowing what to expect. But upon reaching the door, she noticed that it was slightly open and decided to enter. What she saw inside surprised her, there was an elderly lady sitting in a chair next to the fireplace. The lady looked at her and asked what she was doing there. Amelie explained that she had lost her way due to the snowfall and had found this house. The lady offered her to come in and warm up a bit, and Amelie gratefully accepted.

While they drank hot chocolate together, the lady began to tell Amelie about her life, how she had lived alone in that house for so many years, and how she had survived the adverse nature and extreme cold. Amelie listened attentively, fascinated by the lady's stories.

But soon, the snow stopped and Amelie knew she had to go home. The lady gave her a goodbye hug and gave her a rose she had grown herself. Amelie promised to come back and visit her in the future.

After returning home, Amelie shared her adventures with her family and friends, and never forgot the story of the lonely lady who lived in the snowy mountain. She learned that kindness and amiability can be found in the most unexpected places, and that sometimes older people have the most interesting stories to tell.

ACTIVITY

Write a name for the elderly lady Amelie met:

....

....

....

....

....

COLOR AND DECORATE

Get inspired by other creations on social media using #WEAREALLAMELIE

KINDNESS

Designed by Freepik

GOODNESS

54

NO ONE IS BETTER THAN ANYONE ELSE

Amelie has always been a very sensitive girl who cares about others, so when she saw that there was so much competition and rivalry among her classmates, she felt very bad. She knew that this was not good for anyone, and she wanted to find a way to make all her friends understand that all people are equal, and no one is better than anyone else.

One day, Amelie decided it was time to act. She realized that she had to find a way to show her classmates that inclusion and diversity are very important values, and that they should be respected by everyone. So she planned an adventure that would take them on a journey through the forest near her village.

The adventure began with great excitement, and as they walked through the forest, Amelie and her friends found a great variety of animals, plants, and trees. They were surprised to see how all of them lived in harmony, regardless of their size, shape, or color. It was then that Amelie understood that this was the lesson she wanted to teach her classmates.

When they arrived at a clearing in the forest, Amelie explained to her friends that all living beings in nature were equal, and that none was better than any other. She told them that they should learn from nature, and accept others as they are, regardless of their differences.

Amelie's classmates were impressed with her lesson, and began to understand that inclusion and diversity are important values that should be respected. Amelie had achieved her goal, and all her classmates returned home with a new perspective on life and people.

Since then, Amelie has become an example for her classmates and for all the children in her village. She had shown that anyone can be a leader and a defender of inclusion and diversity, regardless of their age.

COLOR AND DECORATE

Get inspired by other creations on social media using #WEAREALLAMELIE

DIVERSITY

Designed by Freepik

INCLUSION

LOVE NATURE AND ANIMALS

On the morning of the field trip, Amelie and her schoolmates were very excited. They had been planning this day for weeks and it had finally arrived. After a short walk, they arrived at a very old bridge that crossed a river. All the children looked down and saw the crystal clear water and rocky bottom.

"Can we cross the bridge?" Amelie asked her teachers.

"Of course," one of them replied, "just be careful and hold hands with your classmates to help each other."

The children began to walk on the bridge, but suddenly, something strange happened. Amelie and her friends began to feel a soft, fresh breeze and when they looked up, they realized they had entered a magical world.

The magical world was full of life and colors. The trees were taller and greener, the flowers were brighter, and the animals were different from the ones they had seen before.

Amelie and her classmates were amazed. Then, suddenly, the animals started to talk.

"Hello!" said a bird, "How are you today?"

The children looked at each other, incredulous.

They couldn't believe that the animals were talking to them.

"We're fine," Amelie replied, "Why can you talk?"

"Because we're in a magical world," the bird replied, "where everyone can understand each other."

The children spent the rest of the day learning about the nature and animals of this magical world. They discovered the importance of taking care of the environment and treating animals with love and respect.

At the end of the day, the children crossed the bridge again and returned to their world, but they will never forget the lesson they learned in the magical world. Amelie and her classmates pledged to be better people and to take care of nature and animals

From that day on, Amelie will always remember the importance of learning about nature and working together to make a better and more sustainable world.

ACTIVITY

Make a list of things you would like to do to help make the world better and more sustainable.

For example: "I will start recycling waste in my house by separating it into organic, cardboard, plastics, and glass."

....

....

....

....

....

....

....

....

....

....

....

....

....

....

....

....

....

....

....

....

....

....

....

....

....

....

....

....

COLOR AND DECORATE

Get inspired by other creations on social media using #WEAREALLAMELIE

Designed by Freepik

UNITED FOR A CAUSE

Amelie had always been a very sensitive girl, concerned about the well-being of others. That's why, when she went to visit her grandmother in the neighboring town, she realized the difficult situation that many people were living in there. Several neighbors were unemployed, many businesses had permanently closed, and a significant number of people did not have access to the basic resources that we all need to survive.

Distressed by this situation, Amelie couldn't just

stand by and do nothing, so she decided to organize a large fundraiser to help the inhabitants of that town. She went from door to door, talking to the merchants in her town and explaining the situation in the neighboring town. They were all moved by Amelie's story and decided to help.

The baker donated fresh bread, the butcher donated fresh meat, the carpenter made toys and furniture, and all the other merchants contributed in some way. They all worked together to organize this great event that would allow them to raise funds for the people in need.

On the day of the fundraiser, the town square was full of people. Amelie had made signs and flyers that explained the serious situation and the importance of helping. The people responded with enthusiasm and generosity, and the fundraiser was a success.

Amelie and her friends took everything they had raised to the neighboring town and delivered it to the people who needed it the most. They were all very grateful and promised that their help would not be in vain.

From that day on, Amelie became a role model in her town and in the neighboring town. She had shown that with a little effort and dedication, it's possible to make a big difference in the lives of others. And, above all, she had taught the importance of helping others and working together for a good cause.

COLOR AND DECORATE

Get inspired by other creations on social media using #WEAREALLAMELIE

Designed by Freepik

OVERCOME THE LOSS OF A LOVED ONE

Amelie had always had a very close relationship with her grandpa Felipe. He was the wisest and most loving man she knew, and she adored him. But one day, after battling a serious illness for many years, Amelie's grandpa passed away.

It was a very hard blow for her, but she knew she had to be strong to support her grandmother and mother who were very sad about what had happened. Amelie decided to focus on remembering the happy moments she had shared with her grandpa and finding ways to honor his memory

She decided to share her story with her friends and classmates at school, and was surprised to see how understanding and kind they were with her. Together, they organized a series of activities in his honor, from a nature walk to a fundraising for a charity organization that fought against the illness that had affected her grandpa.

Thanks to her community and friends, Amelie was able to overcome this tragic event and find peace in his memory. She learned that, although the pain will always be there, she will always have her grandpa in her heart and in her memories. And that the love and support of her loved ones can help her overcome any obstacle.

ACTIVITY

Did you know that July 26 is celebrated as "International Grandparents Day"?

Write a message for all the grandparents in the world telling them how important they are to all children. Share it with your family and friends.

....

....

....

....

....

....

....

....

....

....

....

....

....

....

DRAW, COLOR AND DECORATE.

Make a drawing for the grandparents of the world and ask an adult to take a photo and share it on their social media on July 26 using the #GRANDPARENTSDAY

FEAR OF BEING THE NEW ONE IN CLASS

Amelie was very nervous on her first day at her new school. It was a very large school and she didn't know anyone there. She was afraid of not having any friends, not fitting in with the others, or not being accepted.

However, as her day went on, Amelie began to make new friends. She joined a group of classmates in a school activity and discovered that everyone was friendly and welcoming. Amelie felt more comfortable and relaxed and began to enjoy her classes.

Throughout the weeks, Amelie continued to make new friends and participate in different school activities. She became a more confident and open person. Amelie found in school a place where she could be herself, where she could learn, grow, and be part of a kind and united community.

Amelie realized that it was pointless to be nervous beforehand. It's best to live experiences without preconceptions and let things happen on their own. Life always surprises us and often we will find very good things for ourselves in the least expected places.

In summary, Amelie overcame her fear and found a home in her new school. She learned the importance of making friends and being a good classmate.

ACTIVITY

Write a funny story that you have experienced in school with your classmates:

....

....

....

....

....

....

....

....

....

....

....

....

....

....

COLOR AND DECORATE

Get inspired by other creations on social media using #WEAREALLAMELIE

Designed by Freepik

I AM NOT AFRAID OF SCHOOL

FEAR OF THE DENTIST

Amelie had a terrible fear of going to the dentist. She had heard stories of pain and broken teeth, and simply couldn't imagine someone sticking instruments in her mouth. However, she knew she had to go to keep her teeth healthy and strong.

Her parents wanted Amelie to have a check-up and made an appointment for Friday afternoon. It was Monday and her week would feel endless due to the anxiety and fear it provoked. On the one hand, her fear lingered, but on the other hand, it was better if that appointment never came.

Finally, the day of the appointment arrived, and once at the dental clinic, Amelie was nervous and shaking. But the dentist, a friendly man with a big smile, reassured her and talked to her about the importance of oral hygiene and good nutrition. He showed her how to brush her teeth and use dental floss, and explained why these things were so important.

Amelie was surprised at how easy and pleasant her first visit to the dentist was. At the end of the session, she left with a big smile on her face, and her fear had completely disappeared. From that day forward, she attended her regular dental appointments without any problems and soon became close friends with the dentist.

The dentist encouraged her to keep taking care of her teeth and maintain good oral hygiene. Amelie learned a lot about the importance of keeping her mouth healthy and was always grateful to the dentist for helping her overcome her fear and teaching her how to take care of herself properly.

ACTIVITY

Write down the name of your dentist:

....

Did you know:

It is recommended to have regular dental visits every 6-12 months.

Regular dental visits can not only help with dental health but can also prevent future dental pathologies, cavities, periodontal diseases, among others.

Encourage your parents to make an appointment for a check-up.

COMPLETE

Test yourself. Write the name of all the teeth.

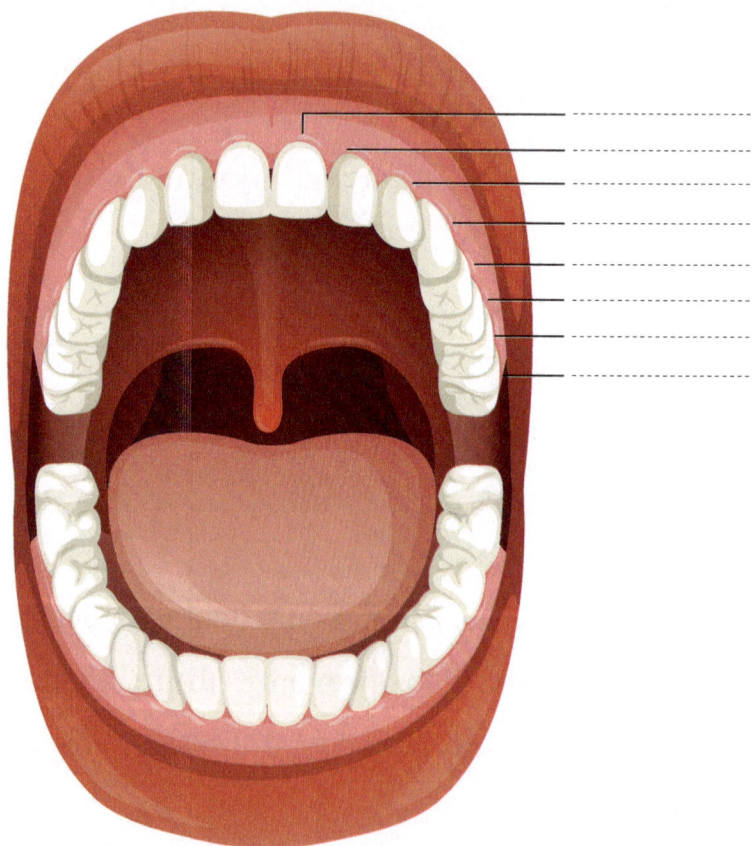

Designed by Freepik

MY PARENTS ARE ARGUING

Amelie had always seen her parents as an inseparable team, they always did everything together. One day, Amelie came home from school and upon entering, she heard a heated argument between her parents. She felt very distressed and didn't know what to do. She imagined her parents separating and having to choose who to live with. This thought filled her with fear and great sadness.

But Amelie didn't want to sit and wait for the outcome, she decided to talk to her parents to see if she could help in any way. It was a difficult conversation, because the parents had not realized that when they argue, the ones who always suffer are the children. After the parents explained to her why they had argued, they were finally able to solve the problem and reassure Amelie that they were not going to separate.

Although the argument had ended, Amelie couldn't stop thinking about those friends who had separated parents. She realized how difficult it must be for them to go through that and felt grateful for having her parents together and happy.

Since then, Amelie values her parents more and tries to help them in any way she can so that they never have an argument like that again. She learned the importance of listening and trying to help others in difficult times and valuing the people we have around us.

ACTIVITY

Make a list of things you can do to help your parents out of love and not obligation:

....

....

....

....

....

....

....

....

....

....

....

....

....

....

....

DRAW, COLOR AND DECORATE

Make a drawing of your family, don't forget yourself. Ask an adult to take a picture and share it on their social media on May 15 using #FAMILYDAY.

I WANT A PET

Amelie had always wanted a pet. She loved animals and dreamed of having a dog to take care of and play with. One day, while walking in the park, she saw a group of children playing with their dogs and felt sad to realize she didn't have one. When she got home, Amelie told her parents about her desire for a pet.

They told her that she had to be very responsible and that a pet required a lot of care. Amelie understood and promised to be the best pet owner. So, together, they went to the animal shelter to find the perfect dog.

When they arrived at the shelter, Amelie was very excited. She saw that there were many beautiful puppies, but one in particular caught her attention. It was a small dog with soft, brown fur. He couldn't stop looking at Amelie with his big, bulging eyes.

Amelie approached him and the puppy began to lick her hand. It was love at first sight. She knew that this puppy would be her perfect companion. But she still had to convince her parents.

Amelie's parents were a little worried because he was a small dog and would require a lot of care. But seeing Amelie's excitement and the love she had for him, they couldn't say no.

So, they took the puppy home and named him "Lucky". Amelie took care of him and loved him with all her heart. Lucky became Amelie's best friend and she never regretted adopting him.

From that day on, Amelie learned the importance of being responsible and taking care of her loved ones, including Lucky, her new pet.

Did you know:

Adopting pets has several benefits, here are a few:

1. Gives a second chance to the pet
2. Unconditional love and companionship
3. Improves mental health
4. Teaches children to be responsible
5. Encourages others to adopt

COLOR AND DECORATE

Get inspired by other creations on social media using #WEAREALLAMELIE

Designed by Freepik

FAR FROM FAMILY

Amelie and her cousin Emma had always been very close. They had grown up together and shared all kinds of adventures and memories. So when Amelie found out that her cousin was moving to another country, she felt very sad and discouraged. It was hard to imagine her life without Emma by her side.

However, she also understood that the move was the best thing for Emma's parents and family. They had been offered a new job abroad with better opportunities and they were very excited for this new beginning.

Despite the pain Amelie felt, she tried to be positive and support her cousin in this new stage. They organized a big farewell party and promised to stay in touch despite the distance.

Amelie learned that life is sometimes difficult and changing, but it also taught her to appreciate the memories and true friendship she shared with her cousin. She knew that this friendship would last forever in her heart, regardless of the distance that separated them.

Over time, Amelie and her cousin wrote to each other constantly and shared their new adventures in different countries. The distance only strengthened their friendship and made them feel even closer to each other.

ACTIVITY

Make a list of cities, countries or places that you know or would like to visit.

....

....

....

....

....

....

....

....

....

....

....

....

....

....

....

....

....

....

ABOUT THE AUTHOR

MILL SNOWS is the pseudonym of an independent author, husband, and father of two teenage children, who has dedicated the last 25 years working in top design, advertising, marketing, and innovation agencies, creating strategies and creativity for large Fortune 500 brands.

His main value has always been to connect and empathize with people and in this case, he shows his great ability to connect with children, creating stories, games, and activities that inspire them.

Now, he has decided to share his experiences with all of us through his book "The Adventures of Amelie", a collection of short stories full of courage, friendship, and inner strength.

Discover the adventures of Amelie and immerse yourself in the magic that MILL SNOWS has created!

SPECIAL THANKS

I would like to express my deepest gratitude and dedicate this book to my beloved children, Bella and Tizi. Their countless experiences throughout their lives have been a constant source of inspiration for the fictional stories contained within these pages, which are all based on everyday life

Furthermore, I extend a special dedication to my cherished wife, Bere, who has been my constant companion and supporter throughout all of life's adventures. She has played an indispensable role in bringing this book to fruition by providing invaluable corrections and suggestions to ensure the highest quality of content

My family's unwavering support and encouragement has been the driving force behind my imagination and the creation of the unforgettable world of The Adventures of Amelie. Thank you for inspiring me and for making my dreams come true.

DRAW, COLOR, AND SHARE IT.

This is a space for you to express your creative freedom and draw freely things or images that have remained in your mind about "The Adventures of Amelie."

Ask an adult to take a photo of your drawings and share them on social media using #WEAREALLAMELIE.

You can also follow @weareallamelie

THANK YOU and see you next time.

DRAW, COLOR, AND SHARE IT

DRAW, COLOR, AND SHARE IT

DRAW, COLOR, AND SHARE IT

DRAW, COLOR, AND SHARE IT

DRAW, COLOR, AND SHARE IT

DRAW, COLOR, AND SHARE IT

Printed in Great Britain
by Amazon

33986108R00059